Jane ADVENTURES

Painting Peril

Written by Trevor Baxendale

Based on the television script 'Mona Lisa's Revenge' by Phil Ford

Contents

Chapter 1
School Trip Surprise

Sarah Jane Smith has a secret job – she saves the world from aliens! She has an amazing computer called Mr Smith in her attic. She also has a sonic lipstick that can open locked doors, make machines work and do lots of other things too.

Sarah Jane has help from her son Luke and his friends, Clyde and Rani.

Luke, Clyde and Rani were on a school trip to an art gallery. Clyde had won a painting competition and this trip was the first prize.

The class was excited about seeing the Mona Lisa. It was the most famous painting in the world and it had just arrived from France.

The owner of the gallery, Mr Harding, was even more excited. He had loved the Mona Lisa all his life. Now it was in his gallery! His assistant, Miss Trupp, was excited too.

"Congratulations on winning the competition," said Mr Harding, shaking Clyde's hand. "Come and see the Mona Lisa!"

As Mr Harding led the class through the gallery, Luke saw a dark wooden box. “Strange kind of art,” he muttered.

“Well, not all artists are as good as Clyde,” replied Rani with a smile.

They walked into a new room.

"Here she is!" announced Mr Harding proudly.

But they were in for a shock. The painting was still on the wall, but Mona Lisa had disappeared! A different face was there instead.

Chapter 2
Meet Mona Lisa

"That's not the Mona Lisa!" cried Clyde.

"Who's that in the painting?" asked Rani.

"That's Miss Trupp, my assistant!" cried Mr Harding. "What's she doing there? Where's Mona Lisa?"

"Right here," said a voice behind them. They turned around to see a woman in flowing, old-fashioned clothes. It seemed impossible, but it was Mona Lisa herself, alive and well! Mr Harding gasped in shock.

"How come you're here?" asked Luke. "And ... walking?"

"I've wanted to get out for centuries, but I've been stuck in that frame!" Mona Lisa explained. "When I came to this gallery, I found I could get out."

"But paintings can't just come alive!" cried Rani.

“They can’t use alien laser blasters either,” Luke added, as he saw the alien blaster in Mona Lisa’s hand.

“That’s the blaster from my painting!” said Clyde.

“Yes, I took it from your painting, but it’s mine now,” smiled Mona Lisa, “so you’d better do exactly as I say!”

"I don't think so!" said a voice from the doorway. Sarah Jane walked into the gallery and pointed her sonic lipstick at Mona Lisa. "Hold it right there!"

"Mum!" smiled Luke, who was very pleased to see her.

"How did you know we needed help?" asked Rani.

"I heard that the Mona Lisa was missing – but it looks like you've found her," said Sarah Jane. "Mr Smith told me that aliens had something to do with this!"

"The Mona Lisa is an alien?" asked Clyde, who could not believe his ears!

Mona Lisa grinned at him. "I'm not an alien," she said, "but I *was* painted with paint made from a rock that fell from Space."

"You mean you're made from alien paint?" asked Luke.

"Alien paint with a mind of its own," muttered Clyde.

Chapter 3
In the Picture

"But ... how did you come to life?" asked Mr Harding. "And why now, when you have been in the painting for 500 years?"

"It's this gallery," answered Mona Lisa. "When I arrived I could feel that something here was ... *different*. There is some kind of alien energy here. It brought me to life."

"Alien energy?" repeated Mr Harding. "In *my* gallery?"

"Help me find where this alien energy is coming from," said Sarah Jane to the others. "Then we can stop it and get her back in her picture for good."

"Maybe it's time I put *you* in the picture!" shouted Mona Lisa. Her hands glowed a fierce red.

Sarah Jane threw her hands up in alarm. In a flash, she vanished.

"Look!" gasped Rani, pointing at one of the paintings on the wall. Sarah Jane was in the painting!

Luke was horrified. He turned angrily to Mona Lisa and shouted, "Get her out of there, *now!*"

"No!" grinned Mona Lisa.

But Rani had an idea. Lying in front of her was the sonic lipstick. Sarah Jane had dropped it just before she disappeared into the painting.

Rani grabbed the lipstick and aimed it at Mona Lisa. The tip glowed red and Mona Lisa cried, "What are you doing?"

"I'm reversing whatever brought you to life," said Rani. "Time for you to go back where you belong!"

Mona Lisa screamed and faded from view. Everyone watched as she appeared back in her frame.

Miss Trupp fell out of the picture and landed on the floor. Sarah Jane fell out of her picture too.

Chapter 4
Alien Art

"Well done, Rani," Sarah Jane said. "Now we need to find out what helped Mona Lisa to get out in the first place, so we can make sure she can't get out again."

Then Luke remembered something he had seen in the gallery. "Mum," he said, "what about this strange wooden box? I knew it wasn't really art!"

Sarah Jane looked at the box. "You're right, Luke – this was made by aliens, not an artist. It's full of alien energy."

She aimed her sonic lipstick once again, and zapped the box.

"Well, I'm glad that's all fixed," said Sarah Jane. "Mona Lisa won't be getting out of her painting again."

"Look at her. She's as pretty as a picture!" smiled Clyde.